Regulation Misled by Misread Theory

Regulation Misled by Misread Theory

Perfect Competition and Competition-Imposed Price Discrimination

William J. Baumol

AEI-Brookings Joint Center 2005 Distinguished Lecture
Presented at the American Enterprise Institute
September 22, 2005

AEI-Brookings Joint Center for Regulatory Studies

WASHINGTON, D.C.

Distributed to the Trade by National Book Network, 15200 NBN Way, Blue Ridge Summit, PA 17214. To order call toll free 1-800-462-6420 or 1-717-794-3800. For all other inquiries please contact the AEI Press, 1150 Seventeenth Street, N.W., Washington, D.C. 20036 or call 1-800-862-5801.

Library of Congress Cataloging-in-Publication Data

Baumol, William J.
    Regulation misled by misread theory : perfect competition and competition-imposed price discrimination / William J. Baumol.
        p. cm.
    Includes bibliographical references.
    ISBN-13: 978-0-8447-1390-8
    ISBN-10: 0-8447-1390-2
    1. Price discrimination. 2. Competition. 3. Antitrust law.
    I. Title.

HF5417.B38 2006
338.6'048—dc22

                                                        2006003184

10 09 08 07 06   1 2 3 4 5

The AEI Press
Publisher for the American Enterprise Institute
1150 17th Street, N.W.
Washington, D.C. 20036

Printed in the United States of America

Foreword

The 2005 AEI-Brookings Joint Center Distinguished Lecture Award was given to Professor Baumol. The purpose of this award is to recognize a person who has made major contributions to the field of regulation and related areas. Senior members of the Joint Center select the distinguished lecturer on the basis of his or her scholarly and practical contributions to the field. The lecturer is given complete latitude in choosing a topic for the lecture.

Professor Baumol is a true Renaissance man. In addition to making seminal contributions to several fields in economics, he is an accomplished painter and sculptor.

The hallmark of Professor Baumol's work is the construction of elegant theory and then exploration of its practical implications. He has made seminal contributions in a number of important areas, including innovation, economic growth, entrepreneurship, welfare economics, and productivity. He even has a disease named after him—Baumol's "cost disease"—which suggests why costs and prices go up relatively rapidly in professions like the performing arts.

In selecting Professor Baumol for this award, the Joint Center highlighted his contributions to the field of industrial organization. One such contribution was to help develop a new theory of "contestable" markets, which recognized that monopoly providers only need the threat of competition to induce them not to exploit their position; a second was to help develop rules that are useful in designing socially efficient regulation, such as the inverse elasticity rule and the efficient component pricing rule; and a third was to help provide a unifying framework for the growing field of environmental economics.

In this monograph, Professor Baumol shows how regulators can be misled by oversimplified economic theory. He focuses specifically on the issue of price discrimination and shows that competitive markets need not result in a single price, contrary to what most of us learned in Economics 101. Professor Baumol then demonstrates a stronger result: Where competitive pressures prevail, they can force all firms to adopt discriminatory prices if consumer arbitrage is difficult. This radically different picture of competitive markets helps explain the near ubiquity of discriminatory pricing in reality and suggests limits to the use of discriminatory pricing as a justification for regulatory intervention.

Like all Joint Center publications, this monograph can be freely downloaded at www.aei-brookings.org. We encourage educators to use and distribute these materials to their students.

ROBERT W. HAHN
Executive Director
AEI-Brookings Joint Center
for Regulatory Studies

ROBERT E. LITAN
Director
AEI-Brookings Joint Center
for Regulatory Studies

Acknowledgments

I am grateful to Daniel Swanson, Janusz Ordover, and an anonymous reviewer for helpful comments and to New York University's C.V. Starr Center for Applied Economics for its support.

The idea for this article was suggested by the illuminating paper by Michael Levine (2002), in which he shows that discriminatory pricing can occur in highly competitive markets. This paper takes the next step and seeks to demonstrate why, under competitive conditions, the firm will normally be forced to adopt discriminatory pricing wherever that is feasible.

I must also express my deep gratitude to the Ewing Marion Kauffman Foundation for its generous support of the research underlying this paper; to Robert Litan, a partner in crime, who arranged for its presentation and publication; to Robert Hahn for his valuable comments; to Richard P. O'Neill of the Federal Energy Regulatory Commission, whose perspicacity led him to ask about the Ramsey optimality of my result at the presentation of this paper at an AEI-Brookings meeting; to Elizabeth Bailey, who, as many times before, saw and pointed out to me the deeper implications of my discussion; to Sue Anne Batey Blackman, who eliminated all barbarity of expression from my earlier drafts; and to Sasha Gentling, who made all the required arrangements with extreme competence and grace.

Regulation Misled by Misread Theory
William J. Baumol

Casual observation suggests that price discrimination is common in many industries that appear to be extremely competitive. . . . [F]irms in the airline, car rental, moving, hotel and restaurant businesses practice common types of price discrimination, and much evidence suggests that high-valuation consumers pay higher average prices than low-valuation consumers. Yet these markets are not characterized by unusually high entry costs, economies of scale, product differentiation, or market concentration.

—Dana, 1998, p. 395

Economists have generally been careful to point out that perfect competition is an artificial concept, albeit a useful and powerful analytic device. But the optimality properties long associated with this market form—and finally analyzed rigorously by Arrow (1951) and Debreu (1959)—have tempted some who are not as careful as they should be to invite regulators and antitrust authorities to use perfect competition theory for guidance in their rulings, as a way to promote the public interest. For example, only this year I heard a conference presentation dealing with the economic and legal principles of copyright suggest that the innovating Schumpeterian entrepreneurs are automatically to be deemed proper subjects for antitrust attention because in the period before imitators enter the market, they can charge prices that exceed the marginal-cost levels of perfect competition. Never mind that this is a prescription for undermining intertemporal efficiency. Never mind that marginal-cost pricing would generally preclude recoupment of the research and development (R&D) costs of the innovations at issue, costs that will have to be incurred many times again if innovation is to continue. And never mind that a world of perfect competition requires constant returns to scale and firms so small that they would never attract the attention of regulators or antitrust personnel. Because perfect competition has been shown in certain circumstances to yield efficient results, it is proposed that the regulated firm be constrained to act accordingly. I have witnessed a multiplicity of regulatory proceedings in which this was at least implicit in the positions taken by some parties to the litigation.

Lest this situation be considered a failing of the poorly educated and, consequently, an infrequent misunderstanding, this paper deals with an issue about which misunderstanding is evidently not so rare—the case of the firm that adopts discriminatory prices. The usually accompanying argument notes that to merit regulatory or antitrust attention, it is frequently required that the target firm be shown to possess monopoly power. But because discriminatory pricing is incompatible with perfect competition, a firm whose prices are discriminatory is, from this fact alone, said to be shown to possess monopoly power.

The purpose of this paper is to show that this ain't necessarily so and that, on the contrary, in a wide variety of instances closer to those that can attract regulatory attention, it is the very presence of effective competition that *forces* discriminatory prices upon the firm.

Specifically, this paper offers a result on the theory of price under competitive conditions that seems not to be widely recognized in the literature and which appears to be directly in conflict with common preconceptions. In brief, this proposition asserts that in a broad range of market types and conditions, where consumers can be separated into distinct groups with different demand elasticities and in which the market's commodity cannot easily be resold by one group to another, market pressures will prevent any equilibrium in which the product price is uniform. Not only will each firm be *forced* to adopt discriminatory prices, but each firm is likely to be forced to adopt a unique vector of prices, each of which is dictated by the market. Thus, this paper seeks to show why price discrimination may occur—and may occur frequently—not despite relative ease of entry (or other competitive pressures) but because of it. In fact, I will show that in highly competitive markets, *firms may have no choice: Competition can force them to adopt the vector of profit-maximizing discriminatory prices.*

Moreover, the second central proposition of the paper argues that, in equilibrium, these discriminatory prices are not haphazard in their welfare properties but will generally constitute a Ramsey optimum—satisfying the second-best welfare attributes of revenue-constrained economic welfare. Neither conclusion means that the public interest requires all industries that employ discriminatory prices to be exempted automatically from regulation. But it does imply the converse: that such industries should not automatically be deemed appropriate objects of regulatory oversight.

A scenario that is by no means rare in regulatory hearings will help convince the reader of the relevance and real pertinence of the central argument. Imagine that a firm serves two markets, I and II, at identical prices p; that ease of entry keeps its profits to zero; and that initially a rival enters market I but not market II. To survive in market I, the firm is forced to reduce its price in that market to $p_1 < p$, leaving the price in market II unchanged; together, the two prices yield no more than zero profit. Now suppose the rival decides to leave market I and enter market II, forcing the incumbent to reduce its market II price to $p_2 < p$, but in order to hope to earn zero profit in total, the firm is forced to raise its market I price, perhaps back again to p. Then it is at least arguable that all three of the prices, p_1, p_2, and p, are competitive and entail price taking rather than price making. Yet the entire scenario is easily misunderstood as "window-shade pricing": temporary and predatory price cuts by the incumbent follow the entrant wherever it may choose to operate, in an attempt to drive that entrant from the market. The purpose of the following discussion is to throw light on such issues.

Neither of the two central propositions here requires any complex reasoning, let alone sophisticated mathematics for its derivation. Indeed, the underlying arguments are basically quite intuitive and elementary. In retrospect, they may even seem obvious, although somewhat disturbing.

I. A Few Remarks on the Price Discrimination Literature

As is generally recognized, price discrimination was first discussed extensively in the French literature. Systematic analysis of the firm under perfect competition and the suggestion that its equilibrium is characterized by uniform pricing can be ascribed to Antoine-Augustin Cournot (1839, chap. VIII). The extensive formal literature on price discrimination had its origins in the work of Jules Dupuit (1854), which made its appearance barely one and a half decades later. As early as the middle of the nineteenth century, Dupuit recognized that price discrimination is a nearly ubiquitous phenomenon—that it is the rule, rather than the exception: "There is almost no industry where this phenomenon is not present" (Dupuit, loc.cit.; also cited in Ekelund and Hébert, 1999).[1] Although Dupuit emphasized the virtual universality of discriminatory pricing, he tended to associate the phenomenon with impediments to competition. Formal analysis of the subject continued in the well-recognized work of F.Y. Edgeworth, A.C. Pigou, and Joan Robinson. Neither Pigou nor Robinson explicitly rejects the possibility of discriminatory pricing in the presence of competition, but both authors confine their discussions to "discriminating monopoly" (Pigou, 1938, chap. XVII). "Under certain conditions monopolists are able to charge discriminating prices" (Robinson, 1960). In contrast, Edgeworth (1925a, 1925b) discusses the welfare consequences of price discrimination under competitive conditions in two articles; he even speaks "in cases of pure competition [of] the advantages of discrimination" (1925a, 101). But he evidently does not mean perfect competition, because he draws demand curves that are downward sloping. More to the point, he does not direct his discussion to showing that such an equilibrium is possible or even likely under competitive conditions but seems only to assume the possibility, proceeding at once to examine the consequences for consumer welfare.[2]

The literature on the subject continues to grow. For example, Hausman and Mackie-Mason contributed a justly noted article on price discrimination in 1988. In that paper, however, they speak of "the necessary monopoly power for price discrimination to take place" (1988, 245n). A number of papers published toward the end of the 1980s and during the following decade focused on price discrimination in markets with some competitive activity (see, e.g., Holmes, 1989; Armstrong and Vickers, 2001), but most of this focused on oligopolistic competition, in which monopoly power is not necessarily precluded. The illuminating writings of Varian (1989), for example, are ambiguous on the subject, but he does provide a useful summary of the argument that discriminatory pricing requires monopoly power. An extensive sample of the writings on such pricing in the presence of oligopolistic competition is to be found in the Armstrong-Vickers bibliography (see also Stole, 2005). This literature has shown that price discrimination is compatible with some degree of competition. In this paper, however, I go beyond that, asserting that price discrimination can occur when the competitive forces are powerful, and that it is those competitive pressures that force the firm to discriminate and can, in addition, select the vector of discriminatory prices that the firm may have to set in order to survive.

Of course, it has long been recognized that firms will sometimes be forced to adopt discriminatory prices to survive. Particularly in the presence of heavy sunk or fixed costs, it is clear that uniform prices set at any level (and, notably, if they are set equal to marginal costs) will not permit the enterprise to recoup its invested outlays. This phenomenon was noted by Dupuit (1854) and has repeatedly been emphasized by Varian (see, e.g., 1996). It follows, of course, that such prices are sometimes imposed upon the firm rather than adopted voluntarily as a means for extraction of monopoly profits.

Toward the beginning of the 1990s, however, it began to be recognized that, more generally, there need be no inconsistency

between effective competition and discriminatory pricing, as illustrated by the quotation from Dana (1998) at the beginning of this
article. In particular, it was recognized that competition does not
preclude discriminatory pricing (see, e.g., Eden 1990), which
includes, at least theoretically, the extreme form of discrimination in
which sellers manage by sufficiently effective pricing design to keep
for themselves all the net benefits of their sales transactions (called
"first-degree price discrimination"; see the two papers by Ulph and
Vulkan, 2000, 2001).

More recently, two distinguished legal scholars have pointed
out that discriminatory pricing cannot be taken to constitute evidence that the firm in question possesses monopoly power (Levine,
2002; Elhauge, 2003). Levine's central point is that discriminatory
pricing can occur in highly competitive markets. Under common
conditions, firms will adopt price discrimination as their optimal
strategy for recoupment of common costs. Elhauge argues that
price discrimination does not prove the sort of market power that
raises antitrust concerns and that reactive price cuts above
the pertinent costs thus do not necessarily constitute an attempt
to protect market power. Rather, price cuts can be an efficient
response to deviations from the output-maximizing price discrimination schedule in competitive markets.

This paper builds on Levine's analysis and that of other contrib-
utors mentioned above, but it goes on to take the next step and
seeks to demonstrate why, under competitive conditions, the firm
will normally be *forced* to adopt discriminatory pricing wherever
that is feasible. Put another way, uniform pricing is *not* to be taken
as the normal characteristic of equilibrium of the competitive firm.
Rather, the heterodox contention here is that discriminatory pricing
is the normal attribute of equilibrium wherever the demand curves
are not horizontal and wherever it is possible for the firm effectively
to prevent consumers in separable groups with different demand
elasticities from reselling products to one another. Thus, what is
new is the result not only that competition is compatible with such
pricing but that wherever such pricing is feasible, effective competition makes it *mandatory* and, in the extreme case, even determines

each of the discriminatory prices that the firm must charge. If that conclusion is correct, then Dupuit's observation about the ubiquity of such pricing becomes easier to understand.

II. The First Central Proposition: Mandatory Price Discrimination in Separable Markets without Entry Barriers

The analysis of the purely theoretical side of the issue rests on only four assumptions about the pertinent markets:

(1) Firms can enter and exit at low cost and with little delay, doing so whenever there are profits to be earned. Such a market is one I have elsewhere dubbed "contestable." In such a market, evidently, barriers to entry in the Stigler (1968) sense are zero and equilibrium profits must also be zero.

(2) Customers can be divided into different groups with differing demand elasticities (e.g., students, senior citizens), constituting different submarkets with negatively sloping demand curves for the firm.

(3) If members of one such group are offered a pertinent product at a lower price than that available to the members of the other group, it is not feasible for the former to resell their purchases to the latter.

(4) The average cost curves of the firms should be roughly U-shaped, at least in the relevant portion of the loci. This last premise is needed to ensure the existence of a discriminatory equilibrium that is stable and competitive. (Its relevance is shown in Section IV of this paper.)

The second and third premises are, of course, the standard assumptions underlying any model of price discrimination. In addition, this paper assumes throughout that the cost and demand conditions in the pertinent market are such as to result in an equilibrium that is unique.

The first of these assumptions—zero entry barriers and entry whenever profits are available in a market—is, of course, an extreme case. Indeed, interpreted strictly, it rules out sunk costs, because the need to incur such costs does indeed constitute a barrier to entry, imposing risk costs upon the entrant from which the incumbent is immune. More will be said on this subject later.

Aside from the premises just described, no further restrictions are required for the central result. Nothing need be assumed about the magnitudes of fixed and variable costs or the presence or absence of the former, as long as those costs, though fixed, are not sunk once and for all. There is no need for additional restrictions upon the nature of demand, or on the ability of firms to operate in more than a single market, or on their ability to limit the quantities of output they can offer at a given price (because restricted output can, if profitable, be replaced by a rival's entry). Even in the absence of any such assumptions, other than those listed above, we have the result:

Proposition 1. Entry Enforces Discrimination. In a market with no barriers to entry, the firm's equilibrium economic profits will be zero. But if, in addition, a seller can separate its customers into distinct submarkets with different demand elasticities of the firm's submarket demand curves, and the firm can prevent its product from being transferred from one customer to another, the normal assumptions of the theory of the firm will require discriminatory prices if losses are to be avoided, so that equilibrium will entail such prices.

Proof of the proposition follows directly from the basic assumptions listed above. As will be emphasized in the next section, all of the assumptions are quite familiar and appear widely in the literature, even elementary textbooks.[3] Note, however, that the assumed differences among demand elasticities in the different submarkets preclude perfect competition, with its universally horizontal supplier demand curves.

It should immediately be clear, intuitively, that the first three of our four assumptions yield Proposition 1. If the market conditions require the firm to charge its profit-maximizing prices in order to break even, and those prices permit it to do so, then those are the prices it will be forced to select in equilibrium. But if discriminatory prices yield profits higher than those that are possible under uniform pricing, it then follows that the (zero-profit) equilibrium profit-maximizing prices must be discriminatory. Moreover, if the maximum is unique, the firm will be a price taker and will have a unique vector of discriminatory prices, dictated element-by-element by the market. Note, however, that we have so far not made use of the fourth premise—U-shaped average costs—which is needed to consider existence and stability of the competitive, discriminatory equilibrium.

III. Discussion of the Four Assumptions

The four assumptions underlying Proposition 1 require only brief discussion:

(1) *Discriminatory prices normally yield higher profits than uniform prices.* This result is sufficiently well known to require no review. It follows directly from the observation that discriminatory prices are free from the uniformity constraint and therefore yield profits no lower than uniform prices. It is also trivial to show that if customers can be divided into sets whose demand elasticities differ, then the discriminator's profits will always be higher. So the only exception is the set of measure zero, in which elasticities are identical.

(2) *If demand is sufficient, entry will drive economic profit to zero, with full recoupment of common fixed and continuing sunk costs.* Clearly, if the attainable earnings in the market were insufficient to repay necessary total costs, including

any common, fixed, and continuing sunk outlays[4] (such as continuing outlays on R&D), no entrepreneur would find entry attractive. So if market conditions permit firms to cover their total costs, including required sunk costs, entry will not drive profits lower in long-run equilibrium. Similarly, positive economic profits will attract entrants into any market that has no impediments to entry, and this will eliminate those profits in equilibrium.

(3) *Maximum profit equals zero profit.* If the firm's maximum long-run profit were negative, it would clearly have to exit, so sales at the corresponding maximum-profit prices would be inconsistent with equilibrium. Similarly, if prices permitted positive economic profits, firms would adopt them. So, by (2), above, equilibrium requires (as under perfect competition) that the profit-maximizing prices yield exactly zero profit.

(4) *The average cost curves of the firms should be roughly U-shaped.* This, of course, is the usual premise of elementary models of perfect competition and monopolistic competition. Its role will become clear in the following section.

Proposition 1 follows directly from assumptions 1 through 3: Under conditions that cannot be deemed abnormal, firms will be forced by competition to adopt discriminatory prices.

IV. Existence and Stability: Need Entry Undercut Discriminatory Prices, and Can Discriminators Coexist?

The preceding arguments can be expected to raise at least two questions in the reader's mind. First, will not the easy entry, whose frequency in reality has been noted, force prices toward uniformity?

Second, there is the other side of the matter: Will not the discriminating firm be able to take over the market and evolve into a
monopolist? The general answer to both questions is that in some
circumstances, either can happen, but not in the situation described
by our model. These questions also draw our attention to the issue
of existence and uniqueness of the discriminatory equilibrium, an
issue that will not be examined formally here but will be dealt
with intuitively.

To deal with these questions most directly and intuitively, it is
helpful to examine the workings of the model with the aid of
some simple diagrams. To avoid complications, I assume that
there are two customer groups, each with downward-sloping and
linear demand curves, $p_i = AR_i = a^i - b_i y_i$ $(I = 1, 2)$. Hence, their
marginal revenue (MR) will also be linear and have twice the
slope of the demand curves, as shown in figures 1(a) and 1(b) for
submarkets (customer groups) 1 and 2, respectively. As usual, to
find the profit-maximizing decisions for the firm as a function of
its total output in the two submarkets, we add the MR curves
horizontally, to obtain the familiar kinked MR curve for the firm
as a whole (figure 1[c]); profit maximization at any given output
level of the discriminating firm requires MR in the two markets to
be equal.

At low levels of total output, $y = y_1 + y_2$, the firm serves only
the more lucrative submarket, market 1 (the submarket that, at low
volumes, offers a higher MR than is offered by the other submarket
at any output level). But once the amount of output sold in market
1 becomes sufficiently large, say at $y = y^*$, it will pay to supply
some amount of product to submarket 2. From the MR curve for
the two submarkets together, we can derive an AR curve for the
firm as a function of its total output and on the assumption that the
price in each submarket is set so as to maximize the total revenue
derived from that level of y. To the left of y^*, the firm's average
revenue curve will have the usual relationship to submarket 1's MR
curve, both starting at the same point and MR having twice the
downward slope of AR. But at y^*, the firm's AR curve has a downward discontinuity at y^*, as shown, because at higher values of y

FIGURE 1

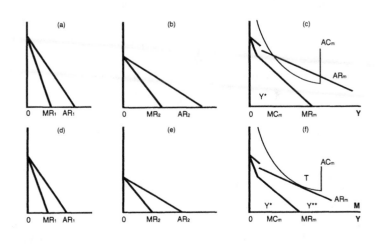

SOURCE: Author's calculation.

the firm obtains part of its revenue from a submarket with lower average returns than the initially served submarket, thereby reducing the average of the returns from the two sources together. Thereafter, to the right of y^*, the AR curve will be linear and will have a slope that is intermediate between those of the AR curves of the two submarkets.

Now, suppose that the average cost (AC) curve for the combined market is as shown by AC_m, part of which lies below the market AR locus, as in figure 1(c). In that case, it is clear that in the absence of barriers, as assumed in the model, entry can be expected to occur. As in the usual story, the result will be a downward (leftward) shift in one or both of the submarket demand curves, which will proceed to the point of tangency, T, between the AR and the AC curves, if such a point exists, as in figure 1(f).[5] Thus, if the curvatures of the average cost and revenue loci are appropriate, there will only be one such tangency point at a unique output level, y^{**}, and at any other output level, the firm will incur losses.

FIGURE 2

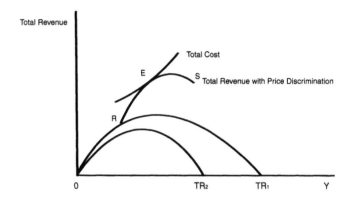

SOURCE: Author's calculation.

Figure 2 shows *total* revenue (*TR*) and cost in the circumstance described in figure 1(f). With the demand curves linear of the form $AR = a - by$, the *TR* curves will satisfy $TR = ay + by^2$. So they will be parabolic, as shown by curves OTR_1 and OTR_2. As before, when total output is small, it will pay the firm to serve only submarket 1, so the *TR* curve for the firm will coincide with that for this submarket. Moving to the right, to larger values of *y*, we reach a point where the slope of OTR_1 equals that of OTR_2, meaning that marginal revenues in the two submarkets are equal at those points; there, it will pay the firm to begin to supply some of its product to submarket 2. From that point onward, the firm's *TR* locus will lie above the OTR_1 parabola to the locus labeled *RS*.[6] The figure also shows an illustrative total cost curve and its tangency point, *E*, with this *TR* curve. Point *E* is the equilibrium point corresponding to that in figure 1(f).

The observation from the two diagrams that is most important to us is that in the situation with which our model deals, at any output other than the equilibrium output at the tangency point in either figure 1(f) or figure 2, the firm will lose money and be unable to survive. This is where our fourth assumption, the U-shaped average cost curve for the firm, comes into play. The diagrams show that with the linear demand curves in the firm's submarkets, this curvature is sufficient to produce that result, although it is not necessary. What is required, clearly, is that the curvature (convexity) of the AC curve be greater than that of the AR curve; that the AC curve contain a downward-sloping segment whose slope (if continuous) decreases in absolute value as y increases from a level initially higher than that of the corresponding point on the total market AR locus; and, finally, that the slope of AC exceeds that of AR.

We are now in a position to answer the two questions posed at the beginning of this section. First, nothing in the equilibrium analysis precludes the existence of a multiplicity of firms that compete in the markets in question. The nature of the cost and demand relationships is such that it prevents expansion of the firm's output level above the equilibrium amount. Consequently, total market demand for the product may well be many times larger than the equilibrium output of the firm. Therefore, a plurality of such firms with similar demands, costs, and equilibrium outputs can coexist, and these outputs can constitute industry equilibrium and can be stable.

Similar reasoning suggests that in such an equilibrium, it will not be possible for the discriminatory pricing to be undermined by a "cream-skimming" entry that attacks only the most lucrative segments of the market. In the circumstances depicted in the graphs, any firm with the same revenue and cost possibilities will incur losses by serving only one market. It follows that even with the competitive pressures that characterize a market having absolute freedom of entry and exit, no force necessarily drives prices toward uniformity.

The argument suggests that, although successful entry into our industry is possible, at least in the unique equilibrium case, only an entrant that opens for business fully grown to the equilibrium output will be able to survive. (Of course, reality is somewhat different, and a few words will be said about that presently.)

We can conclude this part of the discussion with a few remarks on the implications of the discussion for existence and uniqueness of the equilibrium with discriminatory prices. What has been shown here indicates that with little more added (such as continuity of the relevant portions of the derivatives of the AC and AR loci), we can expect such an equilibrium to exist. Uniqueness, however, is a bit more complex. Aside from the obvious possibility of a multiplicity of tangency points, made implausible by the U-shaped AC curve assumption, another complication exists. Along with the discriminatory-price equilibrium, an equilibrium with uniform prices may coexist. Suppose, for example, that the firm has substantial fixed and sunk costs, that two submarkets exist for the firm's product (with profit-maximizing prices $p_1 > p_2$), and that the firm's uniform-price AR curve cuts its AC curve at price $p < p_1$. Then p will evidently be an equilibrium uniform price for the firm, one that prevents entry as a result of the firm's fixed costs and zero profits. Although that arrangement can indeed be a second equilibrium—and one with uniform prices—it is difficult to see why the firm will not take advantage of the opportunity to charge the profit-maximizing discriminatory pricing; doing so will only enhance its earnings temporarily, but that is surely better than nothing. Once the discriminatory price equilibrium has been attained, the profit will be eroded more or less gradually by the threat of entry, and it is difficult to see how the uniform-pricing equilibrium will again come into play.

V. Discriminatory Price Makers or Price Takers?

Some firms with monopoly power, of course, do charge discriminatory prices that yield monopoly profits. But where entry is sufficiently easy, as we have seen, discrimination brings no such profits. More than that, ease of entry deprives the firm of choice in the setting of prices.

The reason for this situation should now be easy to see. For this purpose, we need only consider the likelihood that, in practice, the profit-maximizing price vector for the firm will be unique. If that is so, where that price vector and no other yields zero profits, the firm will have no choice. Any enduring deviation from that vector must be suicidal. The firm will, effectively, be a price taker, although not one that follows a posted price that emerges publicly on a market such as that for, say, pork bellies.[7]

This proposition is not mere theory. In practice, we see marginally surviving firms scrambling for every perceived source of potential revenue and adopting for every such source the price they believe necessary to capture that revenue. Neither the impecunious theater nor the marginal airline can tolerate empty seats. Each seeks desperately to fill them with whoever can help its finances— students, leisure travelers, and others who are unwilling to pay high prices but who will pay a price that contributes *something* in addition to marginal cost. Similarly, that airline cannot forgo the higher price it can impose on business travelers who book at the last minute, because without their contribution to total cost recovery, the firm's financial problems will be exacerbated. To the best of their ability, such firms will select the prices that promise to maximize profits—that is, to minimize losses. Experience may well enable them to come close to selecting the most lucrative prices; if they do not succeed in choosing those prices, they will be replaced by other firms that can do so more effectively.

Thus, market forces impose selection of approximations to the profit-maximizing discriminatory prices. The profit-seeking firm that charges a lower price to union members or to older customers does not do so out of charity but because market conditions force it to do so in order to survive. The supplier firm that charges higher prices for its product when it is sold in the United States than when it is sold in Africa is equally forced to do so. In particular, the airlines that charge higher fares on routes served by few other carriers are not manifesting a monopolist's ability to select an exploitative price. Of course, one cannot doubt that they would want to adopt such lucrative prices if entry were difficult and those prices could bring in substantial economic profits. But even if that were not so, entry would still force them to adopt such prices, whose magnitude is dictated by the rule that maximum profits are zero profits. Discriminatory pricing is not a sign of a breakdown of contestability but rather a manifestation of its normal functioning. If the constraint on profit imposed by entry is potent, the only way for the firm with large fixed and continuing sunk costs to survive will be to engage in price discrimination of the most sophisticated variety that is workable. And only the firm that is more efficient in finding and carrying out better pricing strategies will survive against less creative firms.

The bottom line here is that, where entry is easy, price discrimination is not to be taken as a manifestation of monopoly power.[8] It is true that a monopolist may well be able to engage in price discrimination and that, if it is feasible, the monopolist will generally prefer to do so. But in effectively competitive markets, the same type of pricing can be expected to emerge and to do so as a mandate of the market throughout the industry. The firm that charges discriminatory prices in such an environment is, effectively, a price taker, not a price maker, because no substantial range of prices exists among which management can select. Rather, it is the need to survive that drives those selections, which may well be unique.

Two things need to be said here to adapt this conclusion to reality. First, as noted, in markets of the sort in question it is not unusual for prices to change frequently—indeed, sometimes with astonishing frequency. The fact that the airlines adopt hundreds of thousands of price changes every day can well elicit skepticism about the assertion that these firms have little choice about the prices they adopt. Yet, in the most competitive of markets—the commodity and the securities exchanges—price change is virtually continuous, yet no one is led by this situation to suspect that a relatively small wheat farmer is really a price maker. Indeed, it is mostly in industries where there is reason to suspect that the firms possess market power that prices tend to persist unchanged, often for many months. Sticky prices are not a hallmark of industries in which pricing is controlled by the market.

Lest the reader accuse me of exaggerating, note that unlike a farmer or a purchaser of stocks, the executives in charge of pricing in an airline cannot communicate with any organized market electronically to determine what fares current circumstances impose. They must constantly do their best to determine the current profit-maximizing prices for their firm, but at best they do so imperfectly. They do not have access to current demand functions for their products or even a set of accurate demand functions for some time in the past. Neither they nor anyone else knows their marginal costs or even their average costs, as is confirmed dramatically by examining the records of any substantial antitrust trial in which predatory pricing is an issue. In those trials, in the absence of the pertinent cost data in the records of the firms, specialists on both sides are commonly employed at great expense to determine their own greatly differing and—admittedly imperfectly accurate—cost estimates. Given the unavailability of the requisite information and the speed with which the firm finds it necessary to respond to changing market conditions, the prices selected will, at best, be rather imperfect approximations of the profit-maximizing prices toward which they are driven by market pressures. But that state of affairs is still very different from the leisurely and considered pricing choices available to the firm that is really a price maker, a firm that lack of competition protects from having to obey the dictates that emanate from a powerful market.

VI. Proposition 2: Ramsey Optimality of the Price Taker's Discriminatory Prices

We come now to my second central result:

Proposition 2. Ramsey Optimality. If the profit-maximizing equilibrium that yields zero profit with discriminatory pricing is unique, then it is a Ramsey optimum.

That is, the equilibrium will entail the vector of prices that is Pareto optimal, subject to the constraint that the (expected) economic profits of the firm (and the industry) are zero. The argument is almost trivial. If this is the only set of prices that satisfies the zero-profit requirement, then no other prices can satisfy that constraint and add to consumers'-plus-producers' surplus or can benefit some individuals without harming anyone. That must be true simply because any other price vector, whether better or worse, will violate the constraint. That is all there is to the argument.

We can do a little better than this, however, by deriving the requirements for the equilibrium and showing that they lead to the usual Ramsey formulas. For simplicity, I deal with the case where the marginal costs of serving consumers in the different submarkets are all the same and equal to C' and the demands of the different submarkets are independent, so that all cross-elasticities of demand are zero. Then using obvious notation, equilibrium requires

$$\text{Max} \sum p_i y_i - C' (y_1, \ldots, y_n), \qquad (1)$$

subject to

$$\sum p_i y_i - C' (y_1, \ldots, y_n) = k \text{ (where we will select } k = 0). \qquad (2)$$

The Lagrangian is

$$L = (1 + r)[\sum p_i y_i - C' (y_1, \ldots y_n)] - rk, \qquad (3)$$

where r is the Lagrange multiplier.

But the first-order conditions for maximization of (3) include

$$(1 + r) [1 + (y_i/p_i) \, dp_i/dy_i] = (1 + r) \, p_i \, [1 - 1/E] = (1 + r) \, C' \qquad (4)$$

or

$$(p_i - C')/ p_i = 1/E, \qquad (5)$$

which is, of course, the most elementary form of Ramsey equation.

VII. Proposition 1 and Explanation of
Some Observed Phenomena

Discriminatory pricing is certainly widespread, and its pervasiveness can seem somewhat puzzling. It may be most obvious in passenger transportation, with the complexity of pricing of air passenger transport having become a focus of complaint and even fodder for comedians; "literally hundreds of thousands (!) of [airline] price changes . . . are filed *each day*."[9] But even more common are discounts for students, for senior citizens, for geographically isolated users of telecommunications (in "universal-service" rates), for bulk users of products, for large corporate purchasers of services and inputs, and so on. Indeed, virtually all products whose prices are negotiated between sellers and buyers are sure to entail discriminatory prices. For example, chemical products sold to large firms for further processing are widely negotiated on a customer-by-customer basis. Retailer chains that sell recorded music on CDs and tapes negotiate the substantial fees paid to them by the wholesalers for favorable placement of their releases in retail stores, so that different wholesalers may end up paying different prices for equivalent location of their displays. The list can be expanded substantially to include enterprises such as restaurants (happy-hour drink discounts, pretheater dinner specials,[10] etc.), and theaters (student, senior, union member, and teacher discounts).

But perhaps more surprising is the fact that many of the enterprises that use discriminatory prices appear not to earn profits that exceed competitive levels, despite the monopoly power that is often said to be necessary for the imposition of such prices. This is well known to be true of commercial theaters as a group, in light of their student discounts and the variety of other special deals they offer. The evidence also shows that the major airlines earn, over any substantial period of time, less than the bulk of industries in the economy. Certainly, airline investments earn a lower return than an investment in a comprehensive stock index, such as the S&P 500.[11] Even the computer industry (encompassing both hardware and software), with its widely offered educational discounts and the like, is estimated, as a whole, to have provided no economic profits since its inception. It does of course have its spectacular success stories, but they are apparently fully balanced by the profusion of failures.[12]

We are all aware of the high mortality rate of new restaurants and small theaters. The same is true of new software firms and small entrant airlines. But even the five or six "major" airlines fare no better: In recent years, four of the airlines formerly in this category (Eastern, Pan American, TWA, and Braniff) have expired. Today, United Airlines and America West face great financial difficulties. And Continental and Northwest have undergone bankruptcy, the former repeatedly. Why can these firms, with their demonstrated power to engage in price discrimination, not do better in terms of profits?

Proposition 1 helps dispel the mystery. First, it implies that monopoly power is not required to carry out pricing that is not uniform. Second, the proposition shows that, at least where entry is easy (even if risky), price discrimination not only can fail to yield monopoly profits but, on the contrary, also is necessary to obtain even the minimal competitive profits that such markets offer. The combination of discriminatory pricing and low profits is not a pathological case. It is a normal case wherever customer groups can be partitioned and sold to separately and entry is not difficult.

VIII. Frequency of Entry and Exit in Pertinent Industries with Small but Recurring Sunk Costs

Many of the industries under discussion are characterized by dramatically frequent entry. This is clearly true of restaurants and theaters. Still more striking is the frequency with which start-up software enterprises were, at least until recently, born (and, of course, many of them, like restaurants and theaters, died while very young). And entry is frequent elsewhere. In airlines, the frequency of entry (and exit) is substantial. For example, a witness for the U.S. Department of Justice, whose goal was to provide evidence of possession of monopoly power by the defendant, nevertheless noted that "the top 500 U.S. domestic airline routes experienced 543 entry episodes, over a 6 year period" (Berry, 2000, 3).

If something close to zero economic profit is really the expected ceiling for these firms, the frequency with which they find themselves forced to exit should not be surprising. Such a ceiling does not leave much margin for error. A little inefficiency—that is, efficiency or product quality just a bit less than that of what we may refer to as "best-practice firms"—can then easily be fatal. This story certainly is plausible for restaurants, and there is little reason to doubt that it is far more extensively applicable.

IX. The Role of Regularly Repeated Sunk Costs

The zero-profit attribute of the industry equilibria follows directly for a regime of perfectly free entry, and it is plausible that the attribute is generally approximated where freedom of entry is imperfect but not substantially so. Yet this attribute raises a problem for our discussion related to the effect of sunk costs. Such costs play two different roles that are pertinent for our analysis, but each role appears to offset the other. First, as is generally recognized, sunk costs are the prototypical barrier to entry. If entry requires substantial sunk investment, the risk of entry is increased materially. Moreover, for an incumbent firm a sunk investment is a piece of ancient history, but for a prospective entrant it is a real current cost or an imminent future cost, one that will be incurred if, and only if, entry is undertaken. The incumbent has a substantial advantage because the entrant is subject to a cost from which the incumbent is immune. So a requirement of substantial sunk investment is clearly incompatible with the easy-entry scenario on which the analysis is based.

On the other side of the matter, sunk costs are typically a significant source of the need for discriminatory pricing as a means for the firm to cover its costs. The common, fixed, and sunk costs typically are the reason that marginal-cost pricing will preclude the firm from covering its total costs. Much of the literature on price discrimination (see, e.g., Varian, 1996) does indeed cite fixed and sunk costs as a prime reason forcing firms to eschew uniform pricing.[13] Thus, the apparently contradictory role of sunk costs for our central issue—the market pressures that force firms to engage in discriminatory pricing for survival—are perhaps most likely to derive from the need for sunk outlays by the firm. But such outlays can result in entry barriers whose absence underlies our analysis of the matter.

X. Notes on the Value of the Microtheory of Entrepreneurship and Innovation

On closer inspection, this conflict can largely disappear. The sunk costs that are important for us are not once-and-for-all outlays. Rather, they are continuing expenses typified by the competitive requirement that a firm in a high-tech industry budget for continuous outlays that must be sunk in R&D.[14] As we know, in such an industry, a firm that has once introduced a superior product or an improved production process cannot afford to rest on its oars. The firm knows that it is engaged in a kind of arms race with its rivals; expenditure on further innovation is the prime weapon, and success in the race is ultimately a matter of life and death (on this see Baumol, 2002, part 1).

The sunk costs that traditional theory says do not matter for an incumbent firm's decisions are the once-and-for-all expenditures made in the past and not repeated thereafter. They are the ancient history that no current decision can change, whereas the sunk outlays that the firm *must* be expected to recoup are those that are incurred currently and will continue for the foreseeable future. These expectable and recurring sunk outlays most directly drive the firm to discriminatory pricing. And it is crucial to recognize that they are not barriers to entry in Stigler's (1968) pertinent sense because they are equal burdens for the entrants and the incumbents—that is, they offer no substantial competitive advantage and, hence, no monopoly power to an incumbent firm.

Sunk costs are directly pertinent to the construction of a model that can determine the prices of the services of entrepreneurs, independent inventors, and large firms with substantial R&D activities. With entry into innovative activities largely unobstructed and the big firms driven by an innovative arms race that requires constant investment in the innovation process, we can conclude, first, that they will be driven toward normal profits on their R&D outlays, although the quest for survival will prevent them from abandoning the activity. Second, given the low marginal cost of use of the resulting information, they will be forced to adopt the market-determined discriminatory prices that maximize their profits in order to recoup their R&D investments. Third, by Proposition 2, those prices will tend to be Pareto optimal.

But what about the independent entrepreneurs and inventors? Can a similar story be told for them? The answer, although it may not be obvious at first, is that this story is precisely what the Schumpeterian scenario already has told us, only it has done so in a manner that disguises the price-discrimination side of the story, which precisely follows that just offered for the large, established enterprises. But what is entailed in Schumpeter can be better described as *intertemporal* price discrimination. The entrepreneur and inventor recoup their outlays of money and effort in the initial period after the introduction of an innovation when competition is weak or nonexistent, so the seller's demand curve is inelastic and the profit-maximizing price is high. As imitators appear, the initial seller's demand curve grows more elastic and, consequently, the price falls. The remainder of the story should be clear.

XI. Competitively Enforced Adoption of Means to Segregate Consumers

So far, I have focused on cases that can be considered "natural" candidates for discriminatory pricing—that is, cases in which consumers are readily divided by sellers into different groups to which a given product can effectively be offered at different prices. For some purposes, this targeting is not too difficult, as when customers can be differentiated by sex or age and the products at issue are not easily transferred from one customer to another (e.g., "haircuts" for men and "hair styling," at higher prices, for women). As we know, however, firms are more enterprising than this. They do not leave matters to chance but seek to devise means to separate consumers who otherwise would make their purchases in a single market with a unique product price. After offering a few illustrations, I will show that even in this behavior, the firms are only doing what they are driven to do. Failure to wall off consumer groups from one another where that can readily be done is just as much a threat to survival in a market with no entry barriers as failure to adopt discriminatory prices where market conditions make it easy to do so directly.

Once again, reality provides many cases of such activity. Perhaps the best examples are the many conditions that the airlines impose on their discount fares. For instance, to discourage the use of such options by business travelers, many discount fares require the ticket to span a Saturday night. They hope to exclude business purchasers, who generally have no weekend business meetings at the place they are visiting and who, unlike leisure travelers, are characteristically anxious to get home. The difference in prices between the tickets that cover Saturday night and those that do not is sometimes so great that the business traveler finds it cheaper to purchase two round-trip discount tickets, using (half of) one of them to get to the destination and the other for the return trip.[15] Another example is that of computer printers: slower printers are sold at a lower price than those that are faster. It is reported that in some cases, the two models are, in essence, the same, but manufacturers incur some expense by adding a slowing-down mechanism to the machines intended to be sold at lower prices.

The point is that, once such differentiating measures are discovered, all firms in the market will be obliged to adopt them or some substitute arrangements that induce customers to separate themselves into self-selected purchase groups or that effectively wall off the customers for high-priced sales from the ability to purchase in the low-price segment of the market. The adoption of such a scheme can contribute to profit and constitute a necessary element of a profit-maximizing pricing strategy. Entry, or the threat of entry, will ensure that this new equilibrium arrangement yields only zero economic profit, as the previous and less effective price-differentiating arrangement may once have done but, with a more effective arrangement available, can no longer do.

XII. The Churning Equilibria

If the scenario that has been described here represents a state of equilibrium, one may well ask why, as described earlier, the real markets to which the description is claimed to apply experience so much entry. After all, even a market into which entry is easy and costless will not be highly attractive to potential entrants if the competitive behavior of the incumbents drives economic profits to zero and so offers no special incentive for the creation of new enterprises. But entry and exit do, in fact, occur, and both incumbents and entrants seem to die off with about equal frequency. The equilibria are therefore not stationary, and change does not occur only as a result of exogenous shocks. On the contrary, the equilibria are in a continuous state of churn, and change encompasses not only entry and exit but also the hundreds of thousands of daily price moves that have already been mentioned.

The most obvious inducement for such entry is, first, the fact that an industry whose profits are zero still characteristically contains winners and losers. Entrants can be attracted by excessive optimism or by some special advantage, such as particularly able personnel or a promising new product that leads the entrepreneurs to expect that their profits will be well above the industry norm. Such entrants are often inexperienced, poorly informed, and inadequately financed, and they frequently do not survive.

Second, sunk investment itself often seems to attract niche entrants who skimp on the sunk costs that would enable them to compete with full effectiveness. They hope that they can find a segment of the business in which they can undercut the incumbent and earn a profit by operating there alone; they seek a market in which the incumbents, with their larger recoupment requirements, cannot operate, because the entrants use much less costly plant and equipment. These niche entrants' goal is to survive and accumulate enough to expand their investment, ultimately growing into fully effective rivals. For a variety of reasons, many relating to the entrants' own limitations, they often do not succeed.

Third, the very nature of discrimination would appear to provide entry points for new rivals. The observation that immediately comes to mind, particularly for first-degree price discrimination, in which sellers capture all the available consumers' surplus, is that such pricing seems to make it possible for entrants to offer consumers a better deal than the incumbents are providing. In effect, the entrants are led to believe that they can capture consumers by offering to share with them part of the surplus that the incumbent has commandeered and thereby undermine the discriminatory equilibrium.[16] But if competition has already forced dissipation of the profits—perhaps by forcing down the discriminatory price levels or by bidding up the quantity of expenditure on advertising that current practice in the market requires (i.e., the magnitude of the sunk outlays required for entry)—the discriminator will already have been earning zero profits.[17] In that case, the entrant will have no surplus to share with customers.

A feature of the equilibrium prices themselves appears to make profitable entry possible, and it can tempt entrepreneurs to invade the market. If a firm's prices are not uniform, some of those prices must differ from the firm's marginal costs. Normally, at least some of an incumbent firm's prices must exceed marginal costs in order to permit sunk, fixed, and common costs to be covered. Any market price that exceeds marginal cost and that permits the incumbent firms to earn competitive profits, however, seems to be an invitation for profitable entry through expansion of output. Moreover, the same is true of a price that is below marginal cost, because such a price would appear to make it profitable to enter if the entrant just supplied *less* product than the incumbent in the submarket with the relatively low price. Indeed, one theory is that whenever two or more incumbents offer the same product (among other products) to one given subset of their consumers at the same price, p, that exceeds marginal cost, then profitable entry can occur. In such cases, an efficient entrant whose costs are no higher than those of the incumbents can earn profits higher than those of one of the incumbents (firm S) by adopting prices slightly different from those of firm S.[18] The entrant need merely shave the above-marginal cost prices by a minuscule amount, leaving the essentially unchanged prices still above marginal cost, and sell more than the quantity, y_S, that firm S sold at price p, before entry took place. The entrant can sell this amount, $y_S + k$, without materially depressing the market price, by taking part of its newly acquired business from firm S and part from another incumbent firm, thereby not increasing the total amount sold to the set of customers in question. The entrant must earn more because sale of the additional quantity k will bring in more revenue than it adds to costs, thereby increasing the entrant's profits above the nonnegative profit that firm A was earning before entry.[19]

This proposition can be criticized on theoretical grounds because a profit-maximizing price discriminator will set prices in the submarkets at levels at which *each* marginal cost is equal to *marginal revenue*, whatever the corresponding price, so that expansion of any output should generally reduce profit rather than enhance it. Still, a situation in which some price exceeds marginal cost may well constitute a temptation for the potential entrant, particularly one who is unsophisticated in terms of the underlying economics. And such illusions are readily offset by the risk and uncertainty of entry, including the likelihood of price responses by incumbents and other impediments that together can be expected to require more than a small difference between price and marginal cost before entry actually becomes attractive. Excessive optimism and entrepreneurial propensity to seek out risky ventures, however, can easily work the other way.

The conclusion, then, is that the structure of the equilibria described here can easily invite entry despite the zero expected profits for any pertinent industry as a whole, although one may well question the rationality of the entrants. Those zero profits mean that the market has no room for both incumbents and entrants, so that after entry the demise of some of the firms can confidently be expected. Consequently, constant and unending strategic battle for survival must be common: the time trajectory is characterized by a ceaseless inflow of entrants, followed by a stream of exiting enterprises comprising entrants and former incumbents.

XIII. Conclusion: Implications for Regulation, Antitrust Activity, and Growth Policy

The model described here has substantial implications for regulation, antitrust policy, and issues related to innovation and growth. For regulation and antitrust policy, it appears to offer a drastically revised view of the nature of monopoly power and the evidence that can legitimately be used to support or refute a claim that the incumbents in an industry or some particular firms in that industry possess such monopoly power. For issues related to innovation and growth, the model is significant because so much innovative activity is now carried out by private firms that are characterized not only by relatively low marginal costs of production of their final outputs but also by heavy and continuing sunk outlays on R&D and related activities. Because entry into innovation is often relatively cheap and easy, these circumstances are precisely those in which price discrimination is apt to be indispensable for survival.

The implications of the analysis for rethinking of criteria are illustrated by an ancillary issue: the observation that margins in air passenger transport tend to be higher when a fewer number of carriers serve a given route. This phenomenon has been widely interpreted to imply that in sparsely served routes, the firms possess monopoly power and, more broadly, that the observation refutes the conjecture that the air transport markets are highly contestable. I had previously accepted those conclusions but am now forced to recant. Although passenger air transport may or may not approximate a high degree of contestability, it is clear from the preceding analysis that the empirical observation about the number of airlines serving a route and the magnitude of margins does not help settle the issue. Indeed, in a perfectly contestable market, the cited differences are precisely what should be expected. The smaller the number of airlines that serve a route, the lower one can expect, *ceteris paribus*, the firm's elasticity of demand for service on that route to be. As we have seen, market forces will then make higher margins on that route mandatory. Moreover, besides having little choice on this matter, the frequency of experienced entry indicates that for this and probably other reasons, the airlines cannot expect to derive any monopoly profits in the long run from such pricing. Thus, the firm has no power to extract monopoly profits from these discriminatory prices and no option of setting very different prices without courting financial suicide. It seems hard to conclude, then, either that the firms possess monopoly power or that the airlines operate in markets that are far from contestable.

The implications of this analysis for regulatory and antitrust issues more generally are clear. In a large variety of regulatory-policy discussions, an underlying issue is whether the industry contains firms that have substantial monopoly power. In antitrust hearings, an initial issue that must be settled is whether a defendant firm possessed monopoly power at the time and place in question. If it is determined that the firm had no such power, the case is dismissed because the enterprise is then deemed to have been incapable of carrying out actions that violate the antitrust laws. For this purpose, monopoly power has generally been defined to consist of something such as the "ability to adopt prices that are substantially above the competitive levels and to maintain such super-competitive prices for a substantial period of time." But the analysis presented here calls for modification of this criterion if prices are deemed to be at competitive levels only if they equal marginal costs and only if they are uniform to all customers. This is tantamount to the conclusion that in many industries, the only truly competitive firm is a bankrupt firm.

Rather, the appropriate standard for the evaluation of monopoly power would appear to be the ability of the firm to adopt and maintain a vector of prices that promise *profits* substantially above the competitive level.[20] Other types of evidence can validly bolster or reject a claim that a firm has monopoly power (on this, see

Baumol and Swanson, 2003), but for the purposes of this article it is enough to conclude that price discrimination is not a defensible criterion, because market forces widely impose violation of this standard upon industries that possess no ability to acquire monopoly profits.

The issue is important for economic-growth policy for reasons that have already been noted. Firms engaged in substantial R&D and other innovative activities are, inherently, prototypes of the enterprises on which this paper focuses. It is often relatively easy for new enterprises to embark on innovative activities, in competition with the established firms. Characteristically, firms in those fields dare not fall behind in their continuing and repeated sunk expenditures on innovation. Moreover, the marginal costs of their final products are frequently low, and prices anywhere near those costs are a recipe for financial disaster. The point here is that we must beware of precedents that make such industries targets for regulation and individual firms targets for antitrust prosecution simply because their prices are discriminatory or are not close to marginal costs. Of course, individual innovative firms may or may not behave in ways that violate the antitrust laws, and they should be treated accordingly. But they should not be deemed vulnerable to prosecution simply on the claim that the pricing patterns under discussion show them to be the possessors of monopoly power. Such a course can easily constitute a major handicap to the steadily growing expenditure on innovation by private industry, arguably a mainstay of our economy's unprecedented growth record.

In conclusion, it should be noted that the market's imposition of discriminatory pricing in a wide range of circumstances is not necessarily to be deplored. It has long been known, following Edgeworth (1925a, 1925b) and Pigou (1938), that discriminatory prices can enhance output and increase economic welfare. Recently, Hausman and Mackie-Mason (1988) and Varian (1996), among others, have provided some elegant and powerful results that confirm this observation. And the distributive consequences also (at least sometimes) appear commendable on their face. Low "lifeline rates" that provide electricity and telephone service to impecunious customers, cheaper air fares and theater tickets for students, and a variety of other such arrangements may contribute to the net incomes of the supplier firms, but they can also be accepted as a social benefit that uniform pricing might otherwise preclude.

Notes

1. For a more recent statement, see Carlton (2001): "To recognize how widespread price discrimination is, just think of all the coupons and rebates one gets daily in the mail, newspaper, or just walking down the aisle of any large store."

2. My characterization of the works of these three authors requires some warning. I have not recently reread their entire volumes, so it is possible that I missed some passages that refer to the subjects that I say they did not discuss. But for their main expository material on the theory of price discrimination, the characterizations are offered with confidence.

3. The proposition is foreshadowed by the Baumol, Bailey, and Willig weak-invisible-hand theorem, which asserts that in a monopoly market that is perfectly contestable, the discriminatory Ramsey prices are sustainable against entry. See Baumol, Panzar, and Willig, 1988, chap. 8.

4. The "continuing sunk cost" concept is introduced here only to emphasize that significant sunk costs exist that are not irrelevant to current decisions. Analytically, for the current discussion they need not be distinguished from fixed costs.

5. In figure 1(f), for illustration, the AC curve is evidently one for a total cost that is entirely fixed and provides an absolutely limited capacity to the firm. It should be clear, however, that none of the discussion depends on that premise.

6. Such a heightening of the TR curve will also occur under uniform pricing when the firm begins to serve submarket 2, but the heightened curve will only begin at a level of y greater than that under discriminatory pricing, and the uniform price–heightened curve segment will generally lie below the segment under discriminatory pricing. The second assertion follows from the superior profitability of discriminatory pricing when the cost function is given. In the linear case, the earlier rise in the TR curve under discrimination is also easily shown. Using the equations from above, the equations of the MR curves are of the form $MR = a - 2by$; the vertical axis intercept of the submarket 2 AR curve is evidently a_2; and the slope of the AR curve at that axis is also a_2. Consequently,

with a uniform price the firm will begin to serve submarket 2 when the price in submarket 1 reaches a_2, which will occur when $a_2 = a_1 - b_1 y_1$ or $y_1 = (a_1 - a_2)/b_1$. Under discriminatory pricing, however, submarket 2 will begin to be served when submarket 1's MR falls to that of submarket 2 at the vertical axis, requiring that $a_2 = a_1 - 2b_1 y_1$ or $y_1 = (a_1 - a_2)/2b_1$.

7. Because, so far, only the price-taker side of the firm's activities has been discussed, there is little room for insights from game theory. There is more to the story, however, because the market's equilibria are vulnerable to constant disturbance.

8. On this point, I have my only disagreement with Hausman and Mackie-Mason's excellent and illuminating article, when they speak of "the necessary monopoly power for price discrimination to take place" (1988, 245 n). For the origin of the argument that discriminatory pricing need not require monopoly power, see Levine (2002).

9. Janusz A. Ordover, Initial Expert Report, *U.S. Department of Justice v. AMR Corporation*, 2000 (unpublished).

10. The products are, of course, not perfect substitutes, but the distinctions are introduced by the sellers as a way to divide customers into different groups who can be charged different prices. A clearer example is the division of round-trip airline tickets into those that include a Saturday-night stay at the destination and those that do not.

11. I am, of course, not claiming that easy entry is the only reason, or even the most important reason, for low earnings by the airlines. For example, rising fuel prices have clearly substantially aggravated their financial difficulties. See Joseph P. Kalt, Initial Expert Report. *U.S. Department of Justice v. AMR Corporation*, 2000 (unpublished).

12. "'The computer industry hasn't made a dime. . . . Intel and Microsoft make money, but look at all the people who were losing money all the world over. It is doubtful the industry has yet broken even,' said Peter Drucker in a recent interview. . . . [B]ut is it true? Paul Gompers of the Harvard Business School and Alan Brav of the University of Chicago . . . looked at companies that went public from 1975 to 1992, most of which were high-tech firms, and found their rate of return to be about average [i.e., zero economic profit], once they adjusted for risk and company size." (Katz, 1996).

13. Of course, the primary reason firms adopt discriminatory prices is to increase profits (or reduce losses). But the need to incur sunk and fixed outlays can supplement this influence powerfully if such prices are indispensable for survival.

14. It must be admitted that the high-tech industries do not seem to have been nearly as successful as the airlines in differentiating their prices among customers. Still, extensive school and student discounts for computers and

software and negotiated terms with large corporate purchasers are examples in which the sellers do what they can to use discriminatory prices.

15. This is hardly a new phenomenon. Thus, note Dupuit's 1854 observation, as quoted in Ekelund and Hébert (1999, 217): "On Sunday there is a [train] trip for 10 francs, which during the week costs 50, but what precautions must be taken to prevent one from doing business on a pleasure trip!"

16. I am indebted to my colleague, Lawrence White, for drawing this argument to my attention. For discussions of competitive markets under first-degree price discrimination, see Ulph and Vulkan (2000, 2001).

17. On dissipation of rents such as those offered by discriminatory pricing, see, e.g., Fudenberg and Tirole (1987).

18. It is the possibility that in a perfectly contestable oligopoly market a price above marginal cost may not be sustainable against entry that leads to the conclusion that any *stationary* equilibrium in such a market must entail marginal cost pricing (see Baumol, Panzar, and Willig, 1988, chap. 11; ten Raa, 1984). But such unsustainability of prices above marginal costs can evidently help produce the churning equilibria under discussion.

19. This proposition as it stands has limited applicability to practice because the opportunity for profitable entry it describes requires the entrant to replicate the incumbent's product line almost completely, and requires incumbents passively to eschew any response to the entry. That is one reason the threat of entry can reduce profits to zero without precluding discriminatory pricing. A formal discussion of the proposition is provided in Baumol, Panzar, and Willig (1988, chap. 11, 317 n).

20. Of course, properly interpreted, this standard should refer to economic profits rather than accounting profits, and one must be under no illusion about the difficulties that beset calculation of the magnitude of those profits.

References

Armstrong, Mark, and John Vickers. 2001. Competitive Price Discrimination. *RAND Journal of Economics* 32: 579–605.

Arrow, Kenneth J. 1951. An Extension of the Basic Theorems of Classical Welfare Economics. *Proceedings of the Second Berkeley Symposium on Mathematical Statistics and Probability*. Berkeley, CA: University of California Press.

Baumol, William J. 2002. *The Free-Market Innovation Machine: Analyzing the Growth Miracle of Capitalism*. Princeton, NJ: Princeton University Press.

———— and Daniel G. Swanson. 2003. The New Economy and Ubiquitous Competitive Price Discrimination: Identifying Defensible Criteria of Market Power. *Antitrust Law Journal* 70 (3): 661–85.

————, John C. Panzar, and Robert D. Willig. 1988. *Contestable Markets and the Theory of Industry Structure*. Rev. ed. San Diego, CA: Harcourt Brace Jovanovich.

Berry, Stephen. 2000. Preliminary Expert Report, *U.S. Department of Justice v. AMR Corporation* (unpublished).

Carlton, Dennis W. 2001. A General Analysis of Exclusionary Conduct and Refusal to Deal—Why Aspen and Kodak are Misguided. *Antitrust Law Journal* 68 (3): 659–84.

Cournot, Antoine-Augustin. 1839, 1897. *The Mathematical Principles of the Theory of Wealth*. New York: Macmillan.

Dana, James D., Jr. 1998. Advance-Purchase Discounts and Price Discrimination in Competitive Markets. *Journal of Political Economy* 106: 395–422.

Debreu, Jacques H. 1959. *Theory of Value*. New York, NY: John Wiley.

Dupuit, Jules. 1854. *Traité théorique et pratique de la conduite et de la distribution des eaux*. Paris.

Eden, Benjamin. 1990. Marginal Cost Pricing When Spot Markets Are Complete. *Journal of Political Economy* 98 (6): 1293–1306.

Edgeworth, Francis Y. 1925a. Differential Pricing in a Regime of Competition. In *Papers Relating to Political Economy*. Vol. 1. London: Macmillan and Co., 100–107.

———. 1925b. Discrimination of Prices. In *Papers Relating to Political Economy*. Vol. 2. London: Macmillan and Co., 404–28.

Ekelund, Robert B., Jr., and Robert F. Hébert. 1999. *Secret Origins of Modern Microeconomics*, Chicago. IL: University of Chicago Press.

Elhauge, Einar. 2003. Why Above-Cost Price Cuts to Drive Out Entrants Are Not Predatory—and the Implications for Defining Costs and Market Power. *Yale Law Journal* 112 (4): 681–827.

Katz, Jane. "To Market to Market." Federal Reserve Bank of Boston *Regional Review*, no. 6 (1996), http://www.bos.frb.org/economic/nerr/rr1996/fall/katz96_4.htm.

Fudenberg, Drew, and Jean Tirole. 1987. Understanding Rent Dissipation: On the Uses of Game Theory in Industrial Organization. *American Economic Review, Papers and Proceedings* 77: 176–83.

Hausman, Jerry A., and Jeffrey K. Mackie-Mason. 1988. Price Discrimination and Patent Policy. *RAND Journal of Economics* 19: 253–56.

Holmes, Thomas. 1989. The Effects of Third-Degree Price Discrimination in Oligopoly. *American Economic Review* 79 (1): 244–50.

Levine, Michael E. 2002. Price Discrimination Without Market Power. *Yale Journal on Regulation* 19 (1): 1–36.

Pigou, Arthur C. 1938. Discriminating Monopoly. In *The Economics of Welfare*. 4th ed., pt. II. London: Macmillan and Co.

Robinson, Joan. 1960. *The Economics of Imperfect Competition*. 2nd ed., chap. 15. London: Macmillan and Co.

Stigler, George J. 1968. *The Organization of Industry*. Homewood, IL: Irwin.

Stiglitz, Joseph E. 2000. Preliminary Expert Report. *In the Matter of the United States Department of Justice v. AMR.*

Stole, Lars A. 2005. Price Discrimination in Oligopoly. In Mark Armstrong and Robert H. Porter, eds., *The Handbook of Industrial Organization*. Vol. III. Amsterdam: North-Holland.

ten Raa, Thijs. 1984. Resolution of Conjectures on Sustainability of Natural Monopoly. *RAND Journal of Economics* 5: 135–41.

Ulph, David, and Nir Vulkan. 2000. Electronic Commerce and Competitive First-Degree Price Discrimination. Technical Report. London: University College, available at http://else.econ.ucl.ac.uk/papers/vulkan.pdf.

———. 2001. *E-Commerce, Mass Customization and Price Discrimination.* Unpublished working paper. London: University College

Varian, Hal R. 1989. Price Discrimination. In Richard Schmalensee and Robert D. Willig, eds., *Handbook of Industrial Organization.* Vol. 1. Amsterdam: North Holland Publishers, 597–654.

———. 1996. Differential Pricing and Efficiency. *First Monday* 1 (2), August 5. Available at http://www.firstmonday.org/issues/issue2/different/.

About the Author

William J. Baumol is the Harold Price Professor of Entrepreneurship, and Academic Director, Berkley Center for Entrepreneurial Studies, Leonard N. Stern School of Business, New York University; and Senior Economist and Professor Emeritus, Princeton University.

J O I N T   C E N T E R

AEI-BROOKINGS JOINT CENTER FOR REGULATORY STUDIES

In order to promote public understanding of the impact of regulations on consumers, business, and government, the American Enterprise Institute and the Brookings Institution established the AEI-Brookings Joint Center for Regulatory Studies. The Joint Center's primary purpose is to hold lawmakers and regulators more accountable by providing thoughtful, objective analysis of relevant laws and regulations. Over the past three decades, AEI and Brookings have generated an impressive body of research on regulation. The Joint Center builds on this solid foundation, evaluating the economic impact of laws and regulations and offering constructive suggestions for reforms to enhance productivity and welfare. The views expressed in Joint Center publications are those of the authors and do not necessarily reflect the views of the Joint Center.